Juicing for Health

The Essential Guide To Healing Common Diseases with Proven Juicing Recipes and Staying Healthy For Life

Table of Contents

Introduction

Since the start of the new millennium juicing has become increasingly popular, with scientists, doctors and celebrities discovering the amazing benefits for weight loss, youthfulness, vitality and most importantly health. Celebrities including Owen Wilson, Mark Teixeira, Blake Lively and Edward Norton started endorsing their juicing lifestyle and millions of people followed their example of clean eating. Juicing allows one to conveniently consume an immense amount of nutrients, infusing the cells with phytonutrients, which would normally require one to eat mountains of fruits and vegetables.

However, besides shedding a few extra pounds of weight, detoxifying, rejuvenating and energizing your body, juicing can provide powerful healing attributes, curing or alleviating arthritis, acne, allergies, celiac disease, cancer and many more diseases.

This book will look at the most common diseases and ailments afflicting millions of people every day and suggest juice recipes containing the fruits and vegetables that have proven to be most beneficial for each particular disease.

However, to truly benefit from the juice recipes, it is wise to reduce your intake of the obvious unhealthy foods and habits, such as processed foods, meats, grains, alcohol, soft drinks, and smoking. Invest in a quality electric juicer or blender. If you decide on a juicer, I recommend the Norwalk Hydraulic Press (if you can afford it) or a less expensive Twin Gear or Masticating juicer. I personally use a Vitamix 5200 blender as I prefer the extra fiber intake. Drink your juice immediately ensuring no loss of nutrients. All fruits and vegetables start losing their nutritional value as soon as you slice through their peel. I also recommend purchasing only organic fruits and vegetable to avoid toxic herbicides. Depending on your preference of liquidity of your juices, add one to three cups of filtered water to each juice recipe.

Juicing is effective when done as a juice-only diet, but can also be a very powerful supplement of protective and disease/infection curing nutrients and vitamins to your regular diet, assuming you already have healthy eating habits.

Specific juices are beneficial for healing specific diseases and conditions. I am writing this book with the intention to provide you a comprehensive guide of juice remedies for the most common ailments and diseases.

Thank you again for downloading this e-book. I hope you will greatly benefit from the insights and juice recipes listed below and will feel the positive transformation of your body and mind.

Acne

Lemon Twist (morning drink)
Ingredients
- 1 Lemon
- 1 cup hot water

Carrot Clear
Ingredients
- 8 Carrots
- 2 stalks Celery
- ½ cup Watercress

Dandelion Leaves Juice
Ingredients
- 1 handful Dandelion leaves
- 1 Apple
- 1 Red Beet
- 1 Lemon

Explanation
Acne is an inflammatory disease of the sebaceous glands and hair follicles of the skin that is marked by the eruption of pimples or pustules, especially on the face. Fresh lemon, dandelion, carrots, celery, beets and apples purify the blood, removing metabolic waste and changing pH from acidic to alkaline

Allergies

Red Velvet
Ingredients
- 4 Carrots
- 2 stalks Celery
- 1 cup Pineapple
- 1 thumb Ginger
- ½ Red Beet

Green Beast
Ingredients
- 2 Apples
- 3 stalks Celery
- 1 Cucumber
- 1 thumb Ginger
- ½ Lemon (with rind)
- 1 Lime (with rind)
- 1 bunch Parsley
- 2 cups Spinach

Explanation
Allergies are triggered where the responses to allergens that your body absorbs from the environment or from your diet, causing heightened immune system responses, usually with inappropriate levels of inflammation or irritation. Pineapple contains the enzyme bromelain, which is widely used by German physicians to treat inflammation and swelling of the nose, ear, and sinuses. Recent scientific research has proven that ginger can be used for therapies of various illnesses due to its antioxidant effects, its ability to inhibit the formation of inflammatory compounds, and its anti-inflammatory effects.

Anemia

Beet Anemia
Ingredients
- 4 Carrots
- 2 stalks Celery
- 2 Red Beets
- 1 handful Blackberries
- 2 oz Lettuce

Explanation
Anemia is a condition where the number of red blood cells or concentrations of hemoglobin are low. Iron is the foundation for hemoglobin, the molecule which is responsible for the transport of oxygen. In Europe, beet juice has been used for centuries as a treatment for anemia, due to its high content of iron, folic acid, Vitamin B1, B2, B6, and vitamins A & C.

Anorexia

Life's Gift

Ingredients

- 1 cup Spinach
- 1 Kale leaf
- 1 cup Watercress
- 1 Apple
- 1 Orange
- 1 Tbsp crushed Sesame seeds

Explanation

Anorexia Nervosa is a serious, potentially, life-threatening, psychological eating disorder. Usually, people suffering from this disease will suppress their urge to eat in order to lose weight in order to satisfy their unhealthy, inaccurate body perception. To introduce an anorexic patient back to a healthy eating routine, it may be a good idea to supplement a light diet with nutritional, high fibrous juices. The amount of calories of the juices can gradually be increased using boosts such as Udo's oil and blended seeds and nuts. Research has shown that the liver along with a zinc deficiency are involved in the onset of this disease, which can be counteracted by consuming fruits and vegetable with high contents of zinc. Spinach, kale, watercress and various crushed seeds (pumpkin, sunflower, sesame and flaxseeds).

Arthritis

Joint Juice 1
Ingredients
- 3 oz of Pineapple
- 6 Carrots
- 1 Lemon
- 1 stalk Celery
- 1 thumb Ginger
- 1 handful Cherries (optional)

Joint Juice 2
Ingredients
- 3 Bananas
- 2 thumbs Ginger
- 2 thumbs Turmeric Root
- 2 cups Stinging Nettles
- 1 Courgette
- 3 Carrots
- 1 Lemon
- 1 pinch Cayenne Pepper

Explanation
Arthritis is characterized by the degradation and wearing out of the cartilage surfaces of the articulated joints. When cartilage loses its smoothness and becomes worn out, movement in the joint may be restricted and result in pain. As mentioned above, fresh pineapple contains the enzyme bromelain, which is approved by the German government to be used as a natural anti-inflammatory substance for swollen and painful joints. Ginger is another great food to add to your juice, as it contains potent anti-inflammatory compounds called gingerols. Research has shown that people with osteoarthritis or rheumatoid arthritis consuming ginger on a regular basis have experienced reduced pain levels and improvements in mobility. Two clinical studies concluded that when administered ginger, 75% of arthritis patients and 100% of patients with muscular discomfort reported relief of pain and/or swelling.

Asthma

Blackberry Melon
Ingredients
- ½ cup fresh Basil
- 1 ½ cups Blueberries
- 1 Kiwi
- 2 pinches Cayenne Pepper (powder)
- ½ Lime
- 5 cups Watermelon

Explanation
Asthma is caused by a constriction of the bronchioles resulting in restricted airways and difficulty in breathing. My best childhood friend suffered with this disease for many years. He would use both the blue and brown Ventolin inhalers between twelve to fourteen times a day. More and more people are diagnosed with this condition and there is no doubt that diet plays a major role. Watermelon contains powerful anti-oxidants, which help reduce toxins within the body, which in turn alleviate asthma attacks.

Blood Pressure (Hypertension)

Garlic Joe
Ingredients
- 4 Carrots
- 4 cloves Garlic

Explanation
According to the Center of Disease Control and Prevention (CDC), high blood pressure – or hypertension- afflicts one in three adults in the United States. High blood pressure is a serious affliction and is commonly called the "silent killer", as it can lead to serious and often fatal conditions. Researchers at The University of Alabama concluded that people who were eating garlic on a regular basis experienced lower blood pressure and cholesterol levels, thus reducing the risk of cardiovascular disease. Garlic contains the powerful allicin compound and hydrogen sulfide (H2S), which are responsible for relaxing blood vessels and thus improving blood flow in the arteries.

Cancer

Pom Pom
Ingredients
- 2 Pomegranates
- 2 oz filtered Water

Abricot Magic
Ingredients
- 3 Carrots
- 1 Red Beet
- 3 Cabbage leaves
- 4 Apricots (keep kernels and dry them, see side note below)

Explanation
Pomegranate is famous for its high antioxidant contents. A study at the UCLA Center for Human Nutrition concluded that pomegranate juice, with its immense anti-inflammatory effects due to ellagitannins, is responsible for the suppression of the growth of prostate cancer. Another study conducted by the American Association for Cancer Research showed that cabbage contains highly anti-carcinogenic compounds, called glucosinolates that decrease cell mutation and DNA damage. The study evaluated women, who ate four or more servings of cabbage per week and found that these women were 72% less likely to develop breast cancer than women not eating cabbage.

Side Note: Apricot Kernels
When breaking the hard Apricot kernel you will find soft kernels inside. It is believed that by consuming these soft, bitter kernels on a daily basis one can prevent and cure cancer. These soft kernels contain a unique compound called Amagdylin, or Vitamin B17, which has shown to work with the immune system in the battle against malignant tumors. Laetrile was created by extracting Amagdylin from the soft Apricot kernels and used in treatment by various cancer clinics around the world. Laetrile has become a highly debated and political subject among Big Pharma and AMA. Please conduct thorough research on this type of therapy. I don't accept any kind responsibility for this therapy's uses and effects.

Candida/Thrush

One Step closer to Health
Ingredients
- 2 cups Spinach
- 1 Tomato
- 1 bunch Coriander
- 1 slice Ginger
- 1 tsp Oregano Oil

Candida Mangler
Ingredients
- 2 Carrots
- 1 Red Beet
- 1 stalk Celery
- 1 thumb Ginger
- 1 Lemon
- 1 clove Garlic
- 1-2 cups filtered Water

Berry Throat Juice
Ingredients
- 2 Carrots
- 1 Red Beet
- 1 stalk Celery
- 1 thumb Ginger
- 1 Lemon
- 1 clove Garlic
- 1-2 cups filtered Water
-

Explanation
Thrush is a fungal infection, which is caused by an overgrowth of the yeast organism Candida albicans. Several remedies to treat the excessive yeast are widely available. The Candida fungus thrives on high-sugar and carbohydrates. To eliminate Candida, it is recommended that you refrain from carbohydrates, thus starving the yeast in your system. Juicing vegetables and fruits such as spinach, carrots and tomatoes, may help you fight yeast and maintain the proper balance of bacteria your body needs to function at its best. Garlic and onions contain sulfur and exhibit high antimicrobial attributes. Ginger helps the digestion and fights the infection.

Celiac Disease

Aloe Soother
Ingredients
- 4 Carrots
- 2 Kale leaves
- 1 oz fresh Aloe

Explanation
Celiac disease is an immune disease in which people experience a gluten insensitivity, causing damage their small intestine. Gluten is a protein found in wheat and related grains, like rye, and barley. Gluten most commonly occurs in food, however other products, such as medication and vitamins may also contain gluten.
The symptoms of celiac disease are different for each individual, ranging from abdominal bloating, diarrhea to fatigue, irritability, weight loss and Attention Deficit Disorder (ADD). A study conducted by Jeffrey Bland, Ph.D. showed that Aloe Vera "promotes great gastrointestinal comfort and improves digestion/absorption".

Cellulite

Celery Cellulite
Ingredients
- 6 stalks Celery
- 1 Lemon
- 1 Cucumber
- 3 Apples
- 1 bunch Parsley

Cucumber Fresh
Ingredients
- 2 Cucumbers
- 2 Zucchinis
- 1 bunch Nettle
- 1 Grapefruit

Explanation
Cellulite is widely believed to be a problem for overweight men and women. However, some experts claim that cellulite has nothing to do with the amount of fat under the skin. Toxins and crystallized waste products accumulating in the inert fat cells seem to make the skin appear lumpy, thus causing cellulite. According to this theory, not only overweight people suffer from cellulite and anyone within the ideal weight range may exhibit skin lumpiness. Rather than purchasing expensive cosmetics that claim to remove cellulite, try building up your immune system in order to flush out these toxins and crystallized waste products. Vegetables and herbs like cucumber, celery, parsley and nettle will be of great benefit.

Cholesterol (elevated)

Green Wonder
Ingredients
- 2 Apples
- 3 Cabbage leaves
- 1 Avocado
- 1 Lemon

Trans Fat Terminator
Ingredients
- 2 Oranges
- 1 Banana
- 1 clove Garlic
- 1 Apple

Explanation
Elevated blood cholesterol is one of the most common problems in the United States, blocking arteries and causing heart attack and stroke. Most, if not all drugs to combat high blood cholesterol on the market today have unpleasant side effects that can cause other problems, such as weight gain, constipation, muscle soreness, etc. The main cause for high blood cholesterol is an unhealthy diet, eating high levels of saturated fat, such as fatty meats, eggs and fried foods. People with obesity and people who are physically inactive are at an even greater risk of high blood cholesterol. Apples are known to have a beneficial effect on blood cholesterol levels. In this case I recommend you to blend the juice in order to drink the pulp. Studies have shown that animals who were given apple juice with the pulp included exhibited drastically reduced cholesterol and triglyceride levels. Including the apple pulp in your juice, and thus including the pectin soluble fiber, you essentially cleanse your blood vessels, flushing out cholesterol deposits. Another useful fruit is Avocado, which not only helps reduce dangerous blood cholesterol levels, but also supplies your body with beneficial HDL. Adding cabbage to your juice will supply your body with important sulfur-based amino acids, further helping reduce cholesterol levels.

Cold, Fever, Flu

Turmeric Heaven
Ingredients
- 2 Apples
- 3 Carrots
- 3 stalks Celery
- 1 thumb Ginger Root
- 2 peeled Lemons
- 1 clove Garlic
- 2 Kiwis
- 4 thumbs Turmeric Root

Flu Buster
Ingredients
- 3 Oranges
- 3 Carrots
- 1 Lemon
- 4 cloves Garlic
- 1 bunch Parsley

Explanation
The Flu and the Cold are both viral infections, usually characterized by congestion, sore throat, sneezing, coughing, headache and fever. People who have the flu are likely to run a high fever for several days and experience body aches, fatigue, and weakness. To nourish your body with natural vitamin C, eat plenty of carrots, oranges and lemons. Garlic is well known as nature's antibiotic. A study conducted on 146 people used garlic supplements to prove its antibiotic effectiveness. After only 3 months, the scientists concluded that garlic was highly effective in preventing the common cold and helping in faster recovery.

Constipation

Bowel Mover
Ingredients
- 3 Apples
- 3 Pears
- 2 Plums
- 2 Figs
- 2 Kale leaves

Explanation

Constipation is characterized by irregular bowel movements and hard to pass stools. Many people in the United States eat a diet void of raw, fresh and live foods, consisting of fruits and vegetables. Eating processed foods high in fat and sugar will leave your body depleted of essential natural fibers, which aid in healthy bowel movements.

Another factor causing constipation is a lack of water intake. which is needed in abundant amounts to help the fecal matter become re-hydrated and softened. Dinking diuretics, such as coffee, tea and alcohol dehydrates the body, by urging you to urinate more liquid than you are taking in.

Apples and pears contain plenty of soluble fiber in the form of pectin, which helps to lubricate the bowel. Mixing apples and pears with plums, prunes and figs will ensure you benefit from their potent laxative effects.

Blending the above recipe on a daily basis will retain the vegetable fiber from the fruits and keep your bowels moving. You can add psyllium husk to help increase bulk and water drawing ability of your stool.

Crohn's Disease (works also for Colitis and IBS)

Colon Soother
Ingredients
- ½ Cantaloupe Melon
- 2 Nectarines
- 2 Carrots
- 1 oz fresh Aloe Vera

Explanation

Crohn's Disease is an autoimmune disorder associated with ulceration, inflammation and stricture along the gastro-intestinal tract. This disease is extremely painful and debilitating.

The cantaloupe melon has a very high beta-carotene content, which can help reduce the inflammation and restore natural health to injured mucosal tissue. Recent research has discovered that nectarine juice effectively combats inflammation in the ileum and colon. Aloe Vera is widely known for its soothing and healing properties, not only of the skin with sunburns, but also inside the body. Lastly, carrot juice has the powerful ability to supply your body with nutrients, without irritating the bowels. Once your colon is healed, I recommend a vegan diet, high in fruits and vegetables, along with daily juices such as the one listed above to provide nutrients with minimal stress on your digestive tract.

Cystic Fibrosis

Fibrosis Clear
Ingredients
- 5 Carrots
- 1 cup fresh Pineapple
- 1 Lemon
- 5 cloves Garlic

Explanation
Cystic fibrosis is a hereditary disease causing thick, gooey mucus to build up in the lungs, digestion system, and other parts of the body. Drinking the above juice recipe is a great way to help alleviate the symptoms by dissolving the mucus, flushing out the bacteria and improving the body's overall health. The enzyme bromelain found in the pineapple literally eats up protein old, weak cells. The Fibrosis Clear juice, when consumed on a daily basis, can significantly help people with Cystic Fibrosis get rid of the mucus and thus reduce the frequency of lung and sinus infections and the regular use of medication.

Depression

Asparagus Elixir
Ingredients
- 4 Asparagus
- 1 Orange
- 1 Carrot
- 1 tsp Hemp Oil

Happy Booster
Ingredients
- 4 cups Kale
- 2 cups Spinach
- 1 cup Broccoli
- 1 cup Blackberries
- 2 Oranges
- 1 Lime

Explanation
Depression can range from mild, brief spells of sadness to severe, chronic clinical depression. Clinical depression is a mental health disorder with symptoms such as feeling empty and tearful, loss of interest in most activities, insomnia, fatigue, irritability and feelings of worthlessness. Diets with high intakes of fruits and vegetables, and thus anti-oxidants, can alleviate the depressive symptoms. Research has shown that, people suffering with clinical depression have a folic acid deficiency causing high blood levels of homocysteine, which is known to interfere with depression recovery. Eating or drinking fruits and vegetables high in folic acid, such as kale, spinach, broccoli, oranges nuts, seeds, sprouts and legumes, can help re-balance homocysteine levels and thus counteract depression.

Diabetes

Green Giant
Ingredients
- 3 cups Spinach
- 4 leaves Cabbage
- 2 Kale leaves
- 1 Avocado
- 1 Pear

Bitter Melon Sweetness
Ingredients
- 3 oz Bitter Melon
- 1 cup Broccoli
- 2 stalks Celery
- 3 oz Lettuce

Explanation
Diabetes is a condition where the pancreas cannot keep pace with supplying the right quantities of insulin to deal with glucose in the bloodstream. Today, we are seeing more and more cases of Type II diabetes, especially in younger people. Children of all ages suffer with Type II diabetes, mostly caused by diets loaded with processed foods and refined sugars. The pancreas is overloaded and exhausted and stops to respond to blood sugar levels., which can lead to sugar-coma and death if not treated.

Cabbage has been found to lower blood sugar levels in Diabetics, making this vegetable a prime ingredient. When preparing juices, caution should be give to ingredients that could rapidly rise blood sugar levels. Using an avocado in your juice can effectively counteract fruit sugars, essentially helping control the release of fruit sugar into your blood stream. It is also recommended to reduce your intake of refined carbohydrates while at the same time increasing your intake of fresh vegetables.

I first discovered bitter melon when traveling through China. Chinese medicine makes great use of this vegetable, which has a bitter and pungent taste. While the taste may not be the greatest, you will feel an immediate rush of energy and well-being after consuming one of these little miracle vegetables. Research at the Garvan Institute of Medical Research discovered four compounds in the juice of bitter melon, able to activate an enzyme that helps transport blood glucose into muscle cells, thus drastically reducing overall blood sugar levels.

Diverticulitis

Banana Vera
Ingredients
- 3 Bananas
- 2 oz Aloe Vera Juice

Cabbage Cleaner
Ingredients
- 6 Cabbage leaves
- 4 Carrots
- 1 Banana
- 1 stalk Celery

Explanation
Diverticula are small pockets in the wall of the digestive tract, caused by the inner layer of the digestive tract bulging through weak points in the outer layer. This condition may gradually get worse and cause several other problems, such as dead tissue formation and peritonitis, requiring surgery.

Juicing made with bananas and Aloe Vera juice cause minimal strain on the digestive tract while at the same time minimizing and easing painful peristalsis. I recommend drinking the Banana Vera juice at least once a day to help reduce the inflammation and assist the healing process of Diverticulitis.

Another great vegetable to help heal the surface of the intestines is cabbage, which can be blended with other fruits and vegetable in order to smoothen its strong effects.

Eczema

Skin Rejuvenator
Ingredients
- 3 Apples
- 1 stalk Celery
- 1 Cucumber
- 1 Avocado

Berry Delight
Ingredients
- 2 Asparagus
- 1 cup Spinach
- 1 cup Blueberries
- 1 cup Elderberries

Explanation

Eczema is a superficial inflammation of the skin characterized by itchy, fluid-filled blisters and dry, flaking skin. While the exact cause of Eczema is unknown it is believed that irritants and toxins trigger an immune system response resulting in Eczema symptoms.

Ingredients, such as apples, asparagus, cucumber, avocado, celery, spinach, and berries alkalize the body and help flush out toxins, helping clear your skin from Eczema.

Gout

Red Flush
Ingredients
- 1 Red Beet
- 2 cups Watermelon
- 1 oz Alfalfa
- 1 Cucumber
- 1 cup Elderberry

Explanation
Gout, a complex form of arthritis, causes severe pain and swelling in joints, oftentimes in the big toe. The cause of Gout is the accumulation of urate crystals in the joints, which trigger the pain attacks. These urate crystals form when the body is oversaturated with uric acid, not being able to dissolve and excrete them. In order to protect your organs the body stores the urate crystals in the joints.

In order to counteract the body's high acidity levels, it is recommended to consume alkaline foods such as watermelon, which has been shown to specifically flush out uric acid, blueberries, red beets, elderberries, kale and alfalfa. The Red Flush recipe will significantly reduce, if not heal Gout, assuming you refrain from consuming high acidic foods, such as steaks, organ meat, seafood, alcohol and sugary drinks.

Halitosis

Angel Breath
Ingredients
- 1 Pomegranate
- 1 Lemon
- 1 clove Garlic
- 1 thumb Ginger

Explanation

Halitosis is the medical term for bad breath, a condition difficult to eliminate through normal oral hygiene techniques, such as flossing or brushing your teeth. Most people with halitosis may never realize they have it until someone informs them of their bad breath.

The only way to stop halitosis is to completely detoxify your body. Drinking juices and plenty of water is highly recommended. The above recipe includes Pomegranate, which has been effectively used for centuries in the Middle East as mouthwash and other medicinal uses, due to its high content of anti-oxidants potassium and vitamin C. Lemon, ginger and garlic are highly effective in detoxifying the body while at the same time acting as natural antibiotic, killing off parasites lodged inside your digestive tract and stimulating the liver for cleansing.

Hypoglycemia

Holy Hypo
Ingredients
- 1 cup String Beans
- 1 cup Brussel Sprouts
- 1 Carrot
- 1 Avocado
- 1 tsp Udo's Oil
- 1 Pear

Explanation
Hypoglycemia is common in people suffering from diabetes and characterized by decreased blood sugar levels due to over-insulating and diet. Symptoms may include dizziness, irritability, hunger, high pulse rate, weakness, sweating, anxiety and inability to concentrate. Obviously these symptoms are quite unpleasant. However, proper diet and a regular juicing routine will ensure you won't have to deal with hypoglycemia. Most recommendations discussed above, under "Diabetes" can be applied to Hypoglycemia. Although diabetics try to avoid high blood sugar levels, so do hypoglycemics, as a sudden spike of blood sugar may trigger an over active insulin response, reducing blood sugar levels to a minimum.

String beans are rich in potassium and help restore the insulin-exhausted pancreas. Brussels Sprouts have alkalizing effects, specifically in the pancreas. This juice will reduce the speed at which fructose will pour into the blood stream. Udo's oil and avocados form a buffer around the fruit sugar molecules, slowing down the absorption rate of the sugars.

Kidney Stones

Cranberry Flush
Ingredients
- 3 cups Cranberries
- 3 cups filtered Water

Explanation
Anyone who has suffered from kidney stones certainly remembers the pain associated with them. Kidney stones form when certain chemicals in the urine become concentrated and form crystals. As the crystals grow bigger and transform into the actual kidney stone they get lodged somewhere, blocking the free flow of urine, causing tremendous pain. To prevent kidney stone formation it is recommended to drink plenty of water, eat calcium rich foods such as figs, dates and kumquats, reduce your sodium intake, limit animal protein in your diet and avoid stone-forming foods, such as beets, chocolate, spinach and nuts.

Cranberry is a great fruit in helping you avoid kidney stones. In a study conducted at the University of Cape Town, scientists discovered that drinking cranberry juice reduced the formation of kidney stones.

Migraine

BCOA
Ingredients
- 2 cups Broccoli
- 1 Cabbage leaf
- 2 Oranges
- 1 Apple

Celery Goodness
Ingredients
- 2 stalks Celery
- 4 Carrots
- 1 cup Spinach
- 1 thumb Ginger
- 1 cup Broccoli
- 1 handful Parsley

Explanation
Migraine is a severe headache with a throbbing pain at the front or side of the head. Before the onset of a headache many people report a visual "aura", lasting for 20 to 30 minutes. Some people may only see the aura without ever experiencing a headache.

According to recent research, people suffering from migraine have elevated levels of plasma phenylalanine, tyrosine and tryptophan, which can be caused by eating carbohydrate- and fat-rich foods. Studies have proven that phenylalanine and tyrosine can form a substance called "tyramine", which can trigger migraine headaches. There are certain foods containing tyramine, such as chocolate, aged cheese, beer, wine and dairy products

Carbohydrate and fat ingestion can also elevate phenylal-anine, tyrosine and tryptophan in the brain. Interestingly, phenylalanine and tyrosine form "tyramine" a substance that can trigger migraine headaches in people who are taking anti-depressants. Foods high in Tyramine, known to trigger migraine are chocolate, beer, red wine, soy sauce, cultured dairy products and fermented foods such as aged cheese.

Copper may also trigger migraine headaches, and again foods high in copper include chocolate, nuts, wheat germ and shellfish.

Detoxifying juices made from apples, spinach, cucumbers, lemon and ginger along with plenty of clear water intake are excellent ways to rid yourself of migraines.

Menopause

Meno Juice
Ingredients
- 2 Apples
- 1 Kale leaf
- 1 cup Spinach
- 1 cup Strawberries
- 1 Carrot
- 1 Orange

Explanation
Menopause happens when a woman stops having menstruation cycles. Hormonal changes during that time period can result in irregular menstruation, hot flashes, mood changes and vaginal dryness. Menopause cannot be corrected right away but it can be stabilized over time through a regular work out routine and nutritious diet.

Juicing with the right combination of fruits and vegetables will provide your body with Phytoestrogens (all plants), Boron (strawberries, tomatoes, grapefruits, carrots, prunes, apples, lettuce and cucumbers) and Calcium (found in broccoli and dark leafy vegetables), which all work to ease the symptoms of Menopause.

Morning Sickness

Papayarama

Ingredients
- 2 Tomatoes
- 1 ripe Papaya

Explanation
Morning sickness affects more than one third of pregnant women during the first three month of pregnancy and may occur at any time of the day, especially when the stomach is empty. Tomatoes are rich in vitamin C, carotene, and protein; all beneficial to skin pigmentation. Ripe papaya has proven to be THE miracle fruit in alleviating morning sickness. Papaya contains papain, which soothes the stomach, cures indigestion, vomiting and nausea. Both tomatoes and ripe papayas have high vitamin A contents, which can protect the pregnant woman from calcium loss and at the same time boost her metabolic balance.

Mucus Congestion/Cystic Fibrosis

Mucus Miracle Drink
Ingredients
- 3 big handfuls of Watercress
- 2 Lemons
- 1 Cucumber

Deep Breath
Ingredients
- 3 stalks Celery
- 1 Cucumber
- 2 thumbs Ginger
- 1 handful Mint

Explanation
Chest congestion is a common symptom of respiratory tract infections (such as the common cold).

Chest congestion is what happens when the mucus membranes that line your airways jump into overdrive. These mucus membranes are attacked and become irritated and inflamed because of some irritant that you have breathed in (dust, bacteria or a virus). Extra mucus with a thick consistency is produced to flush out the intruder.

Watercress is a great blood cleanser, dilating capillaries and oxygenating the blood. Ginger is a great anti-inflammatory helping reduce swollen sinus membranes and assist with clearing sinus passages and sinus pressure.

Osteoporosis

Bone Builder
Ingredients
- 1 fresh Chicory (or Endive/Escarole)
- 2 Carrots
- 1 cup Spinach
- 1 Apple
- 1 handful fresh Mint
- 1 Tbsp ground Sesame Seeds (optional; grind in coffee grinder)

Explanation
Osteoporosis is a disease of the bones, causing them to become weak and brittle with a high risk of fracture during minor falls or movements. Thought to be a risk for post-menopausal women it is now very apparent that it also affects younger people and men. There have been several documented cases where the above juice recipe has restored the bone density to almost normal levels after six months of drinking one pint of this juice on a daily basis. Scientific studies have shown that "fructans", or non-digestible carbohydrates, found in chicory can help the growth of "good" bacteria in the intestines allowing them to better absorb bone growth minerals, such as calcium and magnesium.

Premenstrual Syndrome

Smooth Sailor
Ingredients
- 1 bunch Cilantro
- 3 Carrots
- 1 peeled Lime
- 1 cup Spinach
- 1 Kale leaf
- 1 handful Mint

Cramp Carver
Ingredients
- 1 Kale leaf
- 1 Apple
- 2 Red Beets
- 1 thumb Ginger
- 1 cup Spinach
- 1 Banana
- 1-2 cups filtered Water

Explanation
More than 75% of women suffer from premenstrual syndrome (PMS) usually preceding a menstrual cycle. Symptoms may include mood swings, tender breasts, fatigue, irritability and depression to name a few. Popular advice to ease symptoms during this time is to eat more fruits and vegetables, especially Cilantro (reduces water retention), spinach (fends of breast tenderness and abdominal bloating), Limes and Carrots (help clear pores and prevent acne), kale (controls irritability) and red beets. Eat lean foods before and during your menstrual cycle, which will greatly improve the PMS symptoms.

Prostate (enlarged of inflamed)

Red Miracle
Ingredients

- 8 oz Pomgranate

Explanation

Researchers at the Cancer Center of the University of California Los Angeles studied the effects of pomegranate juice on fifty men who were diagnosed with prostate cancer and whose cancer was still progressing. The study concluded that drinking eight ounces of pomegranate juice on a daily basis slowed the cancer progression four fold in eighty percent of the men. Pomegranates are extremely high in anti-oxidants, polyphenols and isoflavones, which are speculated to play a large part in their beneficial effects on cancer. Pomegranates may also supplement the need for hormonal therapy, which is very taxing on the body.

Psoriasis

Skin Healer 1
Ingredients
- ¼ Watermelon
- 3 Carrots
- 1 Avocado
- 1 ½ cup Radish
- 3 sprigs Watercress

Skin Healer 2
Ingredients
- 5 Carrots
- 1 Red Beet
- 1 Cucumber
- 1 oz Aloe Vera juice
- 1 pinch Cayenne Pepper

Explanation
Psoriasis is a chronic autoimmune skin condition characterized by a fast growth of skin cells on the surface of the skin, resulting in dry red patches covered with silvery scales. Currently there is no cure for this condition. However, certain lifestyle changes may improve the symptoms, such as natural sunlight therapy, preferably at eh Dead Sea, and diet changes. Many people claim that diet plays no part in this disease, which is completely wrong. Juicing carrots, avocado, celery, cucumber, watermelon and wheatgrass along with brazil nuts will replenish your body with essential fatty acids, beta carotene, lecithin, and anti-oxidants allowing your body to strengthen its immune system and clear the skin from scales. Avoid drinking alcohol and stay away from tomatoes, white potatoes, red meat and peppers as these may contribute to flare-ups.

Sore Throat/Strep Throat/Tonsillitis

Berry Throat Juice
Ingredients
- 3 Bananas
- 1 cup Blueberries
- 1 cup Blackberries
- 1 Lemon
- 1 bunch Mint
- 1-2 cups filtered Water

Elder Apple Delight
Ingredients
- 3 Apples
- 2 cups Elderberry
- 1 Passion Fruit (or substitute with Papaya)
- 1 Cucumber

Explanation
Sore throats are commonly caused by bacteria, which live in most people's ears, nose and throat. Streptococcus lives inside your body and is kept under control by your immune system and other friendly bacteria. When the immune system is weakened the opportunistic streptococcus will start to multiply rapidly causing inflammation and infection of the mucosal tissues of the throat.

In order to fight infections in your body, it is recommended to only eat light foods so as not to overburden your digestive system, and juicing alkalizing fruits, berries and vegetables, such as cucumbers (soothing and anti-inflammatory), lemon, apples, elderberries and passion fruit. Prepare warm teas made from garden mint (helps digestion), chamomile (relaxing), sage (antiseptic and astringent) and thyme (antimicrobial, antibacterial) to further help alleviate the symptoms.

Thyroid (overactive, underactive)

Thyroid Juice
Ingredients
- 1 Apple
- ½ cup Pineapple
- ½ Red Beet
- 2 stalks Celery
- 1 Carrot
- 1 Lime
- 1 cup Cranberries

Explanation
The thyroid is a butterfly-shaped gland situated on the lower part of your throat. Its main function is to produce and store thyroid hormones that control your metabolism, heart rate, body temperature, and blood pressure. People may either suffer from hyperthyroidism, in which case too much thyroid hormone is produced, or hypothyroidism (most common), in which case not enough hormone is produced.

People who suffer from an under-active thyroid gland will have low body temperatures, constipation, weight gain, fatigue, slow reflexes and thoughts, hair loss and dry nails and skin. The most common causes of a thyroid condition are the deficiency of nutrients such as iodine and selenium, autoimmune disorders, genetics, stress, and environmental influences.

Eating foods with high vitamin A contents, such as sweet potato, carrots, squash and cantaloupe melon and foods high in anti-oxidative contents, such as pineapple, blueberries, cherries, beets and tomatoes will help balance the thyroid function. Stay away from foods, such as broccoli, sprouts, cauliflower, kale, spinach, mustard greens and cabbage as they can inhibit the thyroid function.

Ulcers

Green Suede
Ingredients
- ½ Cabbage (chop off stem)
- 3 Carrots
- 2 stalks Celery
- 2 Apples

Explanation
Peptic ulcers are painful, open sores that develop in the lining of the stomach or upper part of the small intestine. Freshly squeezed cabbage juice is an ancient home remedy for peptic ulcers. Several medical studies have discovered that raw cabbage juice, if taken on a daily basis could provide fast relief to the painful symptoms and drastically shorten the healing time of ulcer sores as compared to the healing time of ulcers where conventional diet and drug therapies were utilized. Cabbage contains potent elements such as amino acid L-glutamine, S-methylmethionine (vitamin U), glucosinolates and gefarnate, which help safeguard and heal the gastrointestinal lining and protect the liver. The powerful healing and nourishing attributes of cabbage are considered far more potent than commercially available antacids. Glucosinolates in particular, are converted to anti-inflammatory isothiocyanates in the body, which keep the ulcer causing helicobacter pylori bacteria in check.

Urinary Tract Infection (UTI)

UTI Be Gone

Ingredients

- 1 cup Cranberries
- 1 cup Watermelon
- 1 stalk Celery
- 1 cup Blueberries
- 1 cup Fennel

Explanation

Urinary tract infections, commonly called UTI, can be caused by yeast or bacteria (E. coli) entering the urinary tract through the urethra. The infection can move into the bladder and settle into its irritated tissue, which then becomes Cystitis. UTI and Cystitis are characterized by a strong, persistent urge to urinate, burning pain when urinating, frequent urination, and cloudy, strong smelling. Make sure to drink lots of water and consume plenty of onions and garlic, which are antibacterial. Stay away from alcoholic drinks and sugar as these will cause more irritation to your bladder.

Several studies have shown that cranberries are extremely useful in treating urinary tract infections by preventing the bacteria from attaching to the cells of the bladder or urinary tract.

Varicose Veins

Vein Juice
Ingredients
- 1 Bananas
- 1 Orange
- 1 cup Strawberries
- 1 cup Pineapple
- 1 cup spinach
- 1 Kale leaf
- ½ cup Broccoli
- 1 thumb Ginger

Explanation
Varicose veins are swollen, enlarged veins right under the skin, usually found in legs, but sometimes also in other parts of the body. Women, older people, obese people and people who live a sedentary lifestyle are more prone to developing varicose veins. Symptoms include cramps and fatigue in the affected body part. The enzyme bromelain found in pineapples is an effective remedy by preventing the development of hard, lumpy skin found around varicose veins. Dark, green vegetable juices are great at stimulate the production of collagen in our bodies, resulting in strong, and smooth skin.

Elderberry Breeze
Ingredients
- 2 cups Elderberries
- 1 Orange
- 1 cup Strawberries
- 1 clove Garlic
- 1 thumb Ginger

Explanation
A virus is a minuscule protein containing either RNA or DNA that can only reproduce inside the cells of another organism. Viruses can trigger mild to severe illnesses in humans, animals and plants. In humans some illnesses may be as mild as the common flu or as severe and life threatening as Ebola. When your immune system is strong and healthy it effectively combats any intruding virus. However, if the immune system is weakened by toxins eating unhealthy, processed foods, drinking excessive alcohol or using drugs, a virus attack can quickly take hold within your body and cause damage.

Elderberries have been used for centuries to remedy various ailments and they are slowly being rediscovered for their astonishing antioxidant attributes and their ability to improve the immune system. Bioflavonoids found in Elderberries protect the cells within your body against the flu virus. A study conducted in 2007 discovered that people infected with the flu virus who took elderberry juice recovered sixty percent faster than people who did not.

Conclusion

Thank you again for downloading this book.

I hope this book will remain a valuable companion for you and your family as I strongly believe that the above mentioned juice recipes, when consumed on a regular basis, will keep you and your family healthy and ensure a life full of vitality and youthfulness.
I am looking forward to hearing your feedback on how these recipes were able to change your life as they did mine.

Lastly, if you enjoyed reading this book, I would highly appreciate your book review, by clicking this link.

Happy Juicing!

Preview Of 'GMO Free Diet: The Ultimate Guide on Avoiding GMO Foods and keeping Your Family Healthy with a GMO Free Diet'

Busting the GMO Myths

Myth #01: GMOs increase the yield potential of the crop
Truth #01: GMOs DO NOT increase yield potential, they may even decrease yield potential of the crop.
High yield is regarded as a complex genetic potential that is based on multi-faceted genetic function. Therefore, increased yield can never be genetically engineered in any crop. Data obtained by earthopensource.org show that the non-GMO agricultural productivity in Western Europe is much better than the GMO productivity in the US. Agroecological practices and conventional breeding are still considered two of the top reasons for productive agricultural yields.
The US Department of Agricultural has released a report that contradicts this particular myth. According to a USDA report of 2002, 'commercially available, genetically modified crops do not show increase yield potential.' Another report in 2014 stated GE (genetically engineered) has not shown any augmentation in yield potentials. Moreover, the herbicide-tolerant seeds may offer lower yields if they contain BT or HT genes."

Myth #02: GMOs are climate change-ready.
Truth #02: Climate change resistance does not solely depend on plant genetics
GMO producers have claimed again and again that crops, which are genetically modified can withstand any severe weather conditions. However, this is completely false as weather resistance of crops highly depends on the complex and invariable genetic traits. Moreover, conventional breeding of crops is still way far ahead than genetic engineering when it comes to delivering crops that are truly climate-ready. Tolerance to climate change partly lies in agroecological techniques widely used today. Some commonly used techniques to prepare crops in extreme weather situations include diversity crop planting and soil building.

Myth #03: GMOs can help farmers reduce the use of pesticides/herbicides
Truth #03: GMOs prompt the use of more pesticides/herbicides
GMO producers have claimed that the production of GMO crops decreases the use of pesticides. However, this is completely untrue. Herbicide-tolerant GMOs make use of a significant amount of glyphosate-based chemicals (e.g. Roundup), which technically is a herbicide. In other words, the reduced pesticide used is replaced by a massive use of herbicide. Consequently, the growing cultivation of herbicide-tolerant crops has led to the production of 'superweeds'. This so-called 'chemical treadmill' in farming has been proven unsustainable and questionable, particularly for farmers in the southern hemisphere.

Myth #04: GMOs improve the nutrition content of the crops compared to naturally bred produce

Truth #04: GMOs have manifested nutritional side-effects caused by genetic alteration

"Healthier and far more nutritional value in agricultural crops" is the promise of GMO producers. However, there are still no nutritionally enhanced, genetically modified products available in the market. Moreover, due to the miscalculated effects caused by genetic engineering, there are now studies proving that GMO products are far less nutritious than their naturally grown counterparts. 'Biofortified' crops, such as the GM Golden Rice, are still not readily available in the market due to the ongoing toxicological testing.

Myth #05: GMOs can help reduce the risks of food shortage

Truth #05: Food security can only be achieved through agroecological farming

The International Assessment of Agricultural Knowledge, Science and Technology for Development (IAASTD) report in 2008, which was highly supported by 58 countries, points out that GM crops are not the key to food security. Moreover, the report highlights that GMOs cannot be endorsed due to safety concerns, inconsistent yields, and restrictive seed patents. The report also expressed that food security can be achieved through the agroecological system of food production. This report was based on a four-year project sponsored by World Bank and carried out by 400 scientists from 80 different countries.

Click here to check out the rest of GMO Free Diet: The Ultimate Guide on Avoiding GMO Foods and keeping Your Family Healthy with a GMO Free Diet on Amazon.

Manufactured by Amazon.ca
Bolton, ON

19170369R00026